County Council

Libraries, books and more . . .

2 5 MAR 2013

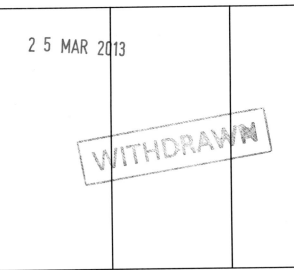
Please return/renew this item by the last due date.
Library items may be renewed by phone on
030 33 33 1234 (24 hours) or via our website
www.cumbria.gov.uk/libraries

Cumbria Libraries
CLIC
Interactive Catalogue

Ask for a CLIC password

Lawrence Sail

Songs of the Darkness

POEMS FOR CHRISTMAS

With illustrations by
Erica Sail

ENITHARMON PRESS

First published in 2010
by Enitharmon Press
26B Caversham Road
London NW5 2DU

www.enitharmon.co.uk

Distributed in the UK by
Central Books
99 Wallis Road
London E9 5LN

Distributed in the USA and Canada
by Dufour Editions Inc.
PO Box 7, Chester Springs
PA 19425, USA

ISBN: 978-1-904634-98-0

Enitharmon Press gratefully acknowledges the financial support of
Arts Council England, London.

British Library Cataloguing-in-Publication Data.
A catalogue record for this book is available
from the British Library.

Designed by Libanus Press
and printed in England by
Antony Rowe Ltd

CONTENTS

FOREWORD

It is over thirty-five years since two poets casually involved me in the writing of Christmas poems. It was either John Mole or Peter Scupham who, in the course of conversation, must have alluded to the seasonal poems they had been writing for a number of years by then, and suggested that I ought to give it a try. I did – only to find that the challenge proved addictive, year on year.

From the outset, there is the matter of fulfilling the commission offered by the event of the nativity. As U. A. Fanthorpe and R. V. Bailey point out in the introduction to the former's *Christmas Poems* (published jointly by Enitharmon Press and Peterloo Poets in 2002), '... trying not to repeat oneself becomes progressively more difficult. The cast, after all, is limited: Virgin, carpenter, baby, angels, wise men'. For U. A. Fanthorpe, part of the solution is to expand the cast somewhat to include, for instance, 'the sheep-dog left behind to look after the sheep while the shepherds were on duty at the manger; the cat who ought to have been there, even if the evangelist failed to notice it; the robin who is somehow, uncanonically, embedded in Christmas.' I, too, have frequently ranged beyond the actual tableau of the nativity to find a sense of the occasion, however tangentially, in landscape, plant life and the calendar, as well as the interplay of hope and history. In this latter regard I suppose that the most obvious antecedents are Hardy's 'The Oxen' and Betjeman's 'Christmas', which introduce a note of dubiety to a context of faith. Auden asserted that all poems are, in effect, commissioned by their makers, and to that extent bound to embody the writer's habitual interests and concerns. So these are poems written for Christmas rather than, without exception, about Christmas.

Not so long after I began writing these annual poems I became editor of *South West Review*, and this came to have a bearing on the matter as well, when the printers of the magazine, Maslands of Tiverton, offered to produce my Christmas cards, complete with envelopes, free of charge each year, as they have continued to do ever since. For this magnanimity I would like to thank Chris May and Andy Jackson – even though, whenever I enquire if they are going to let me off the hook by charging me and so making the whole thing prohibitive, they never do.

I am very grateful to Neil Astley for generously permitting the inclusion here of poems that have appeared in previous Bloodaxe collections; and to Stephen Stuart-Smith of Enitharmon Press for his characteristic care and thoughtfulness. And it is a particular pleasure for me to record my appreciation of the drawings done for a number of the poems by my daughter Erica Sail.

All royalties from sales of *Songs of the Darkness* will be given to Trusts for African Schools, a registered charity which acts as a conduit for money raised in the UK to be sent out to some of the poorest schools in Africa. Its aims are to provide transparent and sustainable development, and to improve the quality of education. No expenses or overheads are paid from donated funds and all administration is conducted free. This means that a hundred per cent of the royalties will reach the local African trusts, and be used for the direct benefit of present and future pupils of the schools. More information, and details of the ten individual schools currently supported by the Trusts, eight in Kenya, and one each in Uganda and Ethiopia, are available on the website www.trustsforafricanschools.org.

L.S.

PROOFS

Delete leaves, the hum of long evenings, light.
Change to bold the grip of frost, black nights.
Rearrange forest gales, seas steep as stairs.
Italicise the stinging slopes of rain.
Stet the murderous world, heartland of despair.
Indent: in the beginning, begin again.

Insert an asterisk over Bethlehem.
Replace damaged characters with wise men.
Substitute stable for inn, manger for bed.
Transpose caviar and crust, fish and hook.
Realign hope, cherish the hungry and the dead.
Print: weigh in your hand spring's budding book.

SLACK

After the long etceteras of the flooding tide,
before the surf rattles back through the beach's knucklebones,
the sea's fallow is as still as the twist of milk
which Vermeer's milkmaid tips slowly and for ever
from a jug to a shallow bowl.

The fishing-boats winched to the top of the shore for winter
lie awkwardly stern on to the steely horizon,
stranded in the damp acoustic of an amnesty
declared between past and future, where all storms
approach as smothered thunder.

Calm of a kind – but unnerving, like the serene
gaze of Piero's pregnant madonna, whose hand
resting on her belly must already feel, above
the unbroken waters, the stirrings of a mortal god,
the hard place of the skull.

CHICKWEED

Simple as any wish –
to take on into winter
such modesty, recalled
from the already dark
verges of summer:
those stars, sparse
and profuse, unparticular
yet keeping measure,
scintillae of the spirit,
white sparks that fly
upward to join
the very idea of spring.

THE CABLECAR

The silver box rose lightly up from the valley,
ape-easy, hanging on by its one arm;
in minutes, it had shrunk the town to a diagram,
the leaping river to a sluggish leat of kaolin,
the fletched forests to points it overrode.
It had you in its web of counterweights,
of circles evolved to parallel straight lines.

Riding the long slurs, it whisked you over
the moraine's hopeless rubble. It had your heart
in your mouth at every pylon, where it sagged,
leaned back, swooped on. It had you hear how ice
cracked on the cable. It had you watch it throw
an already crumpled shadow of bent steel
onto the seracs. It made you think of falling.

By the time it lowered you back to the spread valley,
to the broad-roofed houses decorated with lights,
you could think only of what it was like to step
out, at the top, onto the giddy edge
of snowfields still unprinted, that pure blaze;
to be robbed of your breath by the thin air, by a glimpse
of the moon's daytime ghost on solid blue.

ANNUNCIATION

To anyone looking out beyond
the feverish noise of the city, across
the valley with its twisting path and the lone
cypress close to the bridge, it would be
nothing – a small aperture, one
of several visible in the north wall
of an admittedly fine palazzo.

No hint of the room where a woman
is confronting a creature with wings that crowd
the chequered floor-tiles. Behind the lily
he holds, an arch frames the valley with its bridge
and a nearby tree, and the path twisting
up to the distant city on its ridge –
the world as a miniature nailed to the wall.

SLOES

No lack of present wonders –
the rowan's star-showers
stopped with blood,
the polished ochre
of acorns, some
clamped in their cups,
or the pungent sapwood
locked into each tight bead of holly.

But the darkest amazements of all
in the bright scour
of autumn riches
are the sloes that hang
among wicked spines,
their blue-black skin
misted with a bloom
like breath staying on a flawless mirror.

Cutting one open, you find
a simple pulp
of greeny yellow,
weak moonlight,
and a single nubble
bedded in blister-water,
a bone-hard core,
an oubliette that beggars belief.

From somewhere, the purest birdsong –
last flarings
of the cherished light.
Always you return
to the sloe, to test
the coinage, to conjure
from its sour heart
the future perfect of its white flowers.

ECHO

The year's edge can hardly bear
so much pressure, such stark contests –
between the last door slammed on laughter
and starveling silence, between the glow
of soft tallow and mineral starlight,
between flood and drought, between
darkness unparcelled from gaudy wrapping
and the spick dazzle of the ocean mulling
the next version of itself. Small wonder
that we listen out for a birth-cry of joy –
the seamless ongoing, the way it sounds
beyond doubt, singing in its own echo.

WINTER TRUCES

Between the acidic purities
of boy sopranos scrubbed for matins
and the high web of smothering stone

Between the wind with ice in its teeth
and the low sun of the afternoon
circling behind a framework of trees

Between dark congregations of beet
drilling at dusk on frosty levels
and the cutting edge of a pale moon

Between the longest nights of the soul
and that one star chosen to proclaim
the luxury of a particular God

SONGS OF THE DARKNESS

In the buried darkness
voices are welling
that sing and pray
in a language almost
to be understood.

In the painted darkness
the magi ride onward
with their blazing retinues,
ignoring the huntsman
who aches for blood.

In the darkness outside,
the leprous cities
and lush fields
embody the world
in its broken beauty.

In songs of the darkness
the flowers of the dead
are always in bloom,
and the birth of Christ
is God's first wound.

Yet out of the darkness
come such simple offerings
as ghee, fou-fou
or maize, gifts made kingly
by the recognition of love.

THE GLIMMERING

The horizon draws the line
at having been tamped down
all through a slutchy autumn,
moves in as a caul
of rain which blears the hills,
hissing like the prefix that history
adds to words and laughter:
finally, shrinks to the glimmering
from under a stable door,
a straw-breadth of light which can only
imply the warmth of spring
or the memory of it – the long
pursed buds of the lily
peeling open on the angel's wand.

WINTER SOLSTICE

This is the light least known,
not flashily occulting
or fixed in the sea, steady,
but a deep fire hiding
like a peaty secret sown
at the core of a heath, ready
to burn for as many years
as it takes, the friable ash
collapsing like calcined bone.
This is the true moth-light
by which the eye perceives
the dark dazzle of the earth:
by which the heart believes
it is warmed and not consumed.

CHRISTMAS NIGHT

On the wind, a drifting echo
of simple songs. In the city
the streetlamps, haloed innocents,
click into instant sleep.
The darkness at last breathes.

In dreams of wholeness, irony
is a train melting to distance;
and the word, a delighted child
gazing in safety at
a star solid as flesh.

NATIVITY

They will not be distracted – kings
flipping open jewelled lids,
shepherds bent towards the crib,
the animals safe in their soft gazing.

They seem too blithe, quite unaware
of looming night, as if aloof
under the gleaming fish-scale roof,
as if blind to the world's cares.

Yet they know how we would miss
their wise and quiet attentiveness:
calm as sleeping doves, they bless
the darkness where the stars persist.

LOOKING IN

We might be kneeling down
to the keyhole's angel silhouette,
for a glimpse of a child's room
with its frail silvering starlight:
we might even be spying
on the real ghosts of hope.

They are waiting, perhaps,
beyond our electric clarities:
vivid enough to have lodged
down a far turn of the mind,
sharp enough to prick
our hearts like a lost love.

Ammonite icon of Christmas,
once more your halo franks
the calendar: the old story
locked in your bright chamber
haunts us still as we stare
in, away from the dark at our backs.

A LEAF FALLING

The stem snaps off, brittle
as a wafer – another sycamore
half-star on its way to collapsing
its yellow ribs on the ground.

Not yet: as it slaloms the air
it calls the whole valley to attention –
the glacier's green withheld ghosts,
the breaker's yard of the moraine,
the peaks fat with sunlight.

They attend to a silence which covers
all the leaf's lilting fall:
long enough to contain
the cry of a newborn child
crossing the threshold into
the dazzle, the shadows beyond.

CHAMELEON SONG

Against red – a robin, or Santa's sleeves,
a scatter of peppercorns on oiled green leaves,
or the blood no grief retrieves;

Against yellow – starlight thick as yolk
pouring past the hunched grey headstones, to soak
the grave no birth revokes;

Against brown – public as hope or dust,
soft as a cow's eye, fine as hourglass rust,
time that no heart can trust;

Against blue – the night's tall inky drapes,
the cursive blue of children's dreams, those shapes
no quick feet can escape;

Against all these, though hard to see, may move
the old chameleon, in air still crammed, above
God grounded, the hard rebirth of love.

THE LIGHT AT AGAPIA

This is the light
of a kept secret
inherent and steady
a lily of flame
on a windless night

In an upstairs room
this is the light
at the heart of a country
choking on history's
bitter fumes

Attended by pale
women in black
this is the light
that sharpens the slope
of the hill to be scaled

A deep glow cased
in the grain of the table
the sideboard and chairs
this is the light
no clock can outface

On a winter night
in the presence of death
carried over
like a breath held
 this is the light

Agapia is a convent in northern Romania

FROM THE LARCH

Above a drift of golden needles lying
on sun-dazed snow, bare branches stand embossed
with woody eggs against a fierce blue sky:
impresas apt for God's deciduous birth,
the wordless seed that rises when it dies.

The painters tapped the larch tree long ago,
mixing its turpentine with colour glazes
to model more exactly light and shadow:
the pale bare child, the folds of Mary's dress,
the edge of darkness swirling round the haloes.

ALLOTMENTS IN WINTER

The plots shrink in their drenched sorrows to a scrawl
of husks and hanks, the blackened heads of sunflowers,
with a small flourish of ice-plant here or there,
some bushes dotted with a few berries:
like the sketchy outlines of a story which could in time
acquire the status of a minor classic, whose ending
might be uncertain, but would still give some credence
to delight and the word fleshed in detail –
the ribbing of the wheelbarrow's tyre printed onto mud,
the clang of the spade striking a spark from stone,
the poplars' last highlights that wave all day
from a sky scoured to brightness for tomorrow.

AND THE SHEPHERDS RETURNED

The sheep were waiting,
the same, the equally patient flocks
circling round familiar slopes
or browsing, heavy heads swinging
from inch to inch of nourishment.
Those amber eyes had filtered nothing
in or out: no heavenly host
could separate their days from dreaming.

And they, the shepherds,
came back to every day as simply
as if no star had budged: yet sensed
that lambing, shearing, nursing through
disease and weather, all composed
a calendar of someone's caring.
Even the low vowel of the wolf
came new to them and shaped the darkness.

There was, for them,
no aftermath. What they had seen
became their daily lives, one truth
penned securely inside another.
Now and always they would enjoy
visitant angels and hear, above
the flat bleats of the sheep, voices
pure in praise as hillside water.

THE PUZZLE

And the word made bone was at first
the budding frame of a baby
in its baggy skin:
and dwelt among us, easily
outlasting its quilt of flesh.

In time it also became
evidence beyond contention –
fractured, stove in
or set out on shelves, an index
of bundled tibias and skulls.

Wobble-headed child
of Christmas, supine or propped
on blue, trying
to frown the world into focus,
for you this is yet to come:

the puzzle of how to read
the non-identical twins
of judgement and love,
how to count the broken bones
and still reach out for rejoicing.

WHEN

When in the far deep fathoms
the mackerel lie torpid; when
the hedgehog has curled up and dropped
its heartbeat like a practised yogi

When the balancing seals still float
up to their black air-holes; when
the palolo worm has long since spawned
precisely at daybreak, in Samoa and Fiji

When the poorwill nightjar has gone
to find a rock to sleep in; when
the leaves themselves have counted down
the shortening, shortest hours of daylight

When every triangle is a tree
or half a treetop starburst; when
all threesomes are shepherds, magi
or mother, father and holy child

When to hibernate in a church
might be to dream of hope; even when
outside are only the moon's acid brightness
and cries that carry all through the night

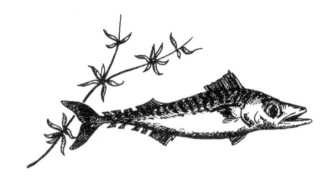

HOLDING-GROUND

A yacht has steered its course
to the calm harbour of the house
where, dressed overall with lights,
it rides the worst of winter,
whole handfuls of baubles
lodged like wind-litter in the rigging:
at the masthead, a leaning star.

The flexible chain that shackles
the hull, paid out by the mind
through crimped wavelets of crêpe,
goes all the way down to the modest
catacomb of the cellar: to the anchor
embedded there, whose outline
twins a cradle and a cross.

A CHRISTMAS CANDLE

It begins as a crackling star
on the soft flesh of tallow,
draws up to a little arch,
burrows a molten pool
tremulous as a tear.

And this recurs, where before
there was only a dull stump,
an opaque pronoun; where the snuff,
black, curled over above
the rim, hung there merely.

Vowel of Christ and child,
its bodied brightness invests
the dark with wild shadows,
the old conspiracies
that hope must still compile.

Though time will bring it down,
it accepts the alighting flame;
though in the night-time draughts
it gutters and sweals, yet
fiercely it burns. Again. Now.

WINTER SONG

These are the names of the dead
which cannot be transcribed –
leaf, blossom, the fledgling love,
the evenings open wide.

This is the land's salt edge
which must not be transgressed –
the tides that mull by a bare crescent,
the damp mantle of mist.

These are the black drum-rolls
that curtain off the stars –
the appalling actual darkness in which
there is still a glimpse, far off,

of the real and imagined dolphins
stitching sea and sunlight,
of the seed resurrected, the bird that soars
on its hot northward flight.

OVERWINTERING

Journeying between
two suns at their closest
to the line clarifies
a point of departure –
the fields where sunlight
softened the stubble,
when the corn was already
scutched and stowed
and the black-bright weave
of the wood still dense
with late leaf-shade.

Ahead, the crocuses
primed for spring
ward their whites,
their light purples –
but long before then,
at a turning-point
where, it is said,
the sun stands still,
a family is waiting,
parents with a child
pale in his stripped innocence.